German Military Ribbon Bars 1914-1957

Mark Hayden

Schiffer Military History
Atglen, PA

Dedication

This book is dedicated to two people: my wife Lorraine, who has tolerated my absences, and still loves me in spite of having to share our home with my ever-present collection of militaria; I also wish to dedicate this book to *Oberst* Adolf Schlicht, a brave German soldier of the Second World War and whom I have come to know and respect over the years. It is through his kindness, self-sacrifice, and support that this book has come to be.

Disclaimer

Every effort has been taken during the preparation of this work to obtain permission from the copyright holders of any photographs used in the book that do not belong to the author. Written permission has been obtained by the author from any copyright holders who could be traced. The pricing of items is in U.S. Dollars and UK Sterling and is accurate at the time of going to press. The prices are based on the items in the condition shown in the photographs.

Book design by Robert Biondi.

Library of Congress Catalog Number: 00-108404.

Printed in China.
ISBN: 0-7643-1206-5

We are always looking for people to write books on new and related subjects. If you have an idea for a book, please contact us at the address below.

Published by Schiffer Publishing Ltd.
4880 Lower Valley Road
Atglen, PA 19310
Phone: (610) 593-1777
FAX: (610) 593-2002
E-mail: Schifferbk@aol.com.
Visit our web site at: www.schifferbooks.com
Please write for a free catalog.
This book may be purchased from the publisher.
Please include $3.95 postage.
Try your bookstore first.

In Europe, Schiffer books are distributed by:
Bushwood Books
6 Marksbury Ave.
Kew Gardens
Surrey TW9 4JF
England
Phone: 44 (0)208 392-8585
FAX: 44 (0)208 392-9876
E-mail: Bushwd@aol.com.
Free postage in the UK. Europe: air mail at cost.
Try your bookstore first.

Contents

Foreword

Having reviewed the organization, format and content of the draft of this book, I was pleased that Mark Hayden chose me to write the foreword.

This reference offers a first time ever in-depth study of a type of regalia which has always been considered a necessary and proud part of the military uniform. This was true throughout the ages to all armed forces around the globe. Ribbons and ribbon bars are a very symbolic and colorful reflection of a soldier's career achievements. Their use and meaning were well known to the individuals who displayed them on their uniforms and also to fellow servicemen. However, up until now, they remained an enigma to collectors of all types of military artifacts.

I personally have been collecting and dealing in military memorabilia for well over three decades. When a fellow collector asks a question about a particular item or topic, I can usually respond with information or at least refer him to a reference book which would provide the necessary and accurate data.

This has not been the case when the question pertained to ribbons and ribbon bars. Mark Hayden's first book has taken a very definite step in the right direction to remedy this void.

It is obvious when reading through this work or trying to locate information on a question one has, that the format and the organization of the materials has been well thought out. Up until now, no reference has dedicated itself to this specific topic. The clear and accurate color images of many elusive, never before pictured, ribbons will delight and inform the viewer. The way that Mark has blended in other anecdotal information on the recipients and even spent some time on the sensitive, but very real topic of reproductions, will not only educate but potentially save the collector from making a mistake in acquiring items to accessorize his collection.

I sincerely believe this reference guide will become a "must have" part of any real collector's library. It is not just the uniform and badge collector who will gain knowledge and insight by having this book at his side. Collectors of any type of German ephemera will benefit as well.

Bill Shea
Hubbardston, MA USA
Summer 2000

Acknowledgments

I wish to thank the following individuals and institutions for their great kindness to me during the course of this project. Were it not for the help, kindness and patience of many of these people, this project would never have appeared as it does now.

Jamie Cross is a well known and highly respected authority on and dealer in Third Reich awards and decorations. As well as being the source of some of the rarer items in my collection, Jamie allowed me to use many items from his own collection, some of which appear in the book. He also helped me greatly with the section on the 1957 awards. He was always happy to chat for hours on the phone, answering some very obscure questions about Imperial ribbons!

Brendan Clarke has collected a vast pictorial collection of the Knight's Cross holders of the German armed forces of World War II. It is thanks to Brendan that I am able to provide a colour photograph of a Bundeswehr officer displaying his 1957 awards in their ribbon form. Brendan also kindly afforded me the use of some of his ribbons of the Iron Cross for the book, notably the 1870 ribbon bow.

Justin Horgan allowed me to use a vast quantity of photographs form his private collection. Justin has been collecting militaria for many years and also turned up some nice ribbon bars of which I am the lucky owner. Justin proved to be a great help with contacting veterans from the various arms of service and obtaining the 'man in the field' experiences of obtaining and wearing ribbon bars.

Derek Jones is a well-known Irish militaria dealer and has now become well known on the Internet also. Derek allowed me to use the picture of *Reichsmarschall* Hermann Göring. Derek has had a long interest in the Luftwaffe of World War II and helped me to track down information on the World Wide Web.

Franco Mesturini is well known in the world of military writing. He has opened his vast collection of military photographs, which range from 1800-1960, to many authors, as well as myself. His own book *Feldgrau*, is an excellent photographic resource of German servicemen and women in uniform throughout World War II.

Franco went to great trouble in sending me photographs of whatever subject I requested, especially the more obscure paramilitary organisations and many World War I studio portraits.

Marineschule Murwik, Flensburg: The Naval History Training Centre of the German Naval Academy at Flensburg, so steeped in maritime history and tradition, were extremely kind to me when I wrote requesting a photograph of *Grossadmiral* Dönitz. I am especially grateful to *Korvettenkapitän* Dr. Hillman who took so much time and trouble to find the photograph I was looking for.

Kevin Conley Ruffner kindly sent me a photograph of a member of a Luftwaffe Field Division which he used in his book Luftwaffe Field division 1941-1945. He received the photograph from Herr Georg Jagolski of the 21st LwFd Association, who is a veteran of the Luftwaffe field Divisions.

Oberst a.D Adolf Schlicht is world famous as one of the leading researchers of the German Army. His *Uniform and Traditions* series of books, co-authored with John Angolia, are a must for collectors and historians alike. Herr Schlicht is a highly decorated veteran of both the Wehrmacht and the Bundeswehr. Without his kindness to me, the section on 1957 awards would not have been possible. His selflessness is an example to us all.

Charles Sharkey has been a long-time friend of mine. His art lies in the realm of photography, and he has done a superb job in taking all of the colour photographs which illustrate this work. An author can only do so much and when I embarked upon this project, Charles took over the photography and came back to me with everything a 100 times better than I could have ever hoped. Thanks to him, a lot of explanation is unnecessary as the pictures speak for themselves.

Bill Shea is well-known in collecting circles as the most honest militaria dealer in business today. He trades under the title The Ruptured Duck and I have come to know and trust Bill completely over the years. He has been a fountain of knowledge and support to me during this project and allowed me to have photographs of a very special ribbon bar indeed, that of *Feldmarschall* Erwin Rommel, 'The Desert Fox' I am delighted to have been able to include such a famous General's awards in this book and it is thanks to my dear friend Bill that this has been possible. He also kindly agreed to write the foreword to this book.

Frank Yeoman (Broadsword Militaria) was the first militaria dealer I ever bought anything from and has remained an honest and resourceful source of militaria since. It is thanks to Frank that I have been able to illustrate this book with so many variations of ribbon bars and bows. Frank ranks highly in that small band of militaria dealers from whom one can buy an item with complete confidence.

Introduction

There have been many works published on the vast subject of German militaria in the years since the end of the Second World War. Practically every aspect of German medals, awards, uniforms and equipment have been covered in many excellent books, videos and magazine articles. However, one area of German militaria that has been neglected is the whole subject of ribbon bars (kleine ordensschnalle). Most books on German soldiers in the Second World War will feature at least one, two, or more photographs of a German soldier, sailor or airman wearing his awards, which will often include a ribbon bar. My interest in this area of collecting began when I bought an M40 German Tunic for an Army enlisted man. The tunic was in good condition and unremarkable apart from the fact that there was a small ribbon bar over the left breast pocket. I purchased the tunic and my curiosity was sparked by the ribbon bar. As I later discovered, it was a common bar – Medal of 13-3-1938 (Austrian Anschluss), and the Medal of 1-10-1938 (Sudetenland Medal) – and was not original to the tunic.

However, I was struck at how much history was contained in so small a piece of militaria and so began my collection of ribbon bars. There are many ribbon bars still available on the collecting market yet in the years that I have been collecting ribbon bars, I have never been able to find a book on their construction, meaning, value and availability. Hence my attempt to provide a book to fill this obvious gap. Ribbon bars may not appear the most desirable items of Third Reich militaria at first glance but when you consider the significance of the awards on a ribbon bar, then you may begin to appreciate their collecting value. A record of a individual's bravery and military service can be discovered quickly by being able to identify the awards on his/her ribbon bar.

It was common practice for German servicemen to wear all of their awards into combat. This was possible with the pin-back awards and qualification badges such as the Iron Cross 1st Class (Eisernes Kreuz 1. Klasse/EK1), Wound Badges (Verwundeten Abzeichen), Assault Badges (Sturm Abzeichen), etc. However, med-

Hauptmann Günther Wrona wearing a ribbon bar consisting of the Iron Cross 2nd Class, Russian Front Medal, Rumanian Anti Communist Service Medal and what may be the Star of Rumania. His other awards are the Knight's Cross, Close Combat Clasp in Bronze, Infantry Assault Badge in Silver and the Wound Badge in Black. *Courtesy of Justin Horgan.*

An Afrika Korps soldier displaying the ribbons of the Iron Cross 2nd Class 1939, 1-10-1938 Medal and the Italian German Campaign Medal. *Courtesy of Franco Mesturini.*

als such as the Iron Cross 2nd Class (Eisernes Kreuz 2. Klasse/EK2), Russian Front Medal (Medaille "Winterschlacht im Osten 1941/42."), and the long service medals (Wehrmacht-Dienstauszeichnungen) would not be practical to wear in their medal form from a concealment and durability point of view. Hence the need for ribbon bars to be worn on the service uniform. As well as from a practical point of view, it was against military law for a soldier not to wear medals and awards to which he was entitled to. The full medals could and were worn on ceremonial or off-duty occasions in the parade or walking-out uniform. They certainly could not be worn in the confines of a U-boat on patrol or in a Panzer IV in the middle of an attack!

As I hope to show during the course of this book, ribbon bars were a means for soldiers to display their medals in a manner that was suited to all environments of military service. I do not even begin to claim that this book is a reference work because I am sure that there are many collectors throughout the world with just as much, if indeed, not more knowledge on the subject of the ribbon bars worn by German servicemen during the Second World War than I have. My aim for this book is to provide a handy guide for collectors who may want to decipher ribbon bars in their own collection, to know what to look for in a ribbon bar, and perhaps to generate an interest in this somewhat neglected area of collecting. I have also included a section on some of the reproduction ribbon bars on the market because, as with most aspects of Third Reich militaria, ribbon bars have also received attention from the ever-present fakers, and those willing to sell bogus items.

one

Wearing the Ribbons

There were three methods of wearing medal awards employed by the German military during the period of 1933-1945. The first method was to wear the actual medal(s) on a medal bar whilst wearing the walking out dress tunic (Tuchrock) or for ceremonial events such as parades, medal awards, funerals, and weddings. The medals would be worn in the court mounted fashion as displayed in the opposite photograph. Generally, this manner of wear was fairly infrequent and as a result, original examples of court mounted medals tend to be in very good condition.

The second method of wear applied only to certain awards. These were as follows; Iron Cross 2nd Class, 1914 or 1939, 1939 Bar to the Iron Cross 2nd Class 1914, War Merit Cross 2nd Class, with or without Swords, Russian Front Medal, Cross of Honour for Valour (Eastern Peoples award). When a ribbon or ribbons were worn in this manner, they were slipped into the buttonhole at the top button of the four button tunic, in the corresponding position on the Luftwaffe fliegerbluse, the second highest button on the five button tunic and on the left lapel of the panzer wrap-over tunic. The Iron Cross ribbon was always worn uppermost, with any other of the aforementioned awards being placed under it. When a ribbon was worn in this manner, as in the photograph on page 14, this ribbon could not be worn on the ribbon bar. However, many soldiers wore ribbons sewn onto their tunic as well as on a ribbon bar i.e. Iron Cross 2nd Class worn in the second buttonhole and also worn on the ribbon bar.

The third method of wear is the one that concerns the subject of this book Ribbon bars were generally worn on the service uniform, along with all the pin-backed awards that the soldier had earned. The ribbon bar was worn over the left pocket of the Waffenrock (Uniform Tunic) of the Heer, the Waffen-SS and the Luftwaffe, as illustrated in the photograph on page 15. Ribbon bars were worn in a corresponding position on the Kriegsmarine pea-jacket, and tunics, and also on the Luftwaffe fliegerbluse, although this was contrary to regulations. However, there is

A Luftwaffe four-pocket tunic for an enlisted man of an anti-aircraft unit. The awards shown are the court-mounted medals of the Iron Cross 2nd Class 1939 and the 1-10-1938 Occupation Medal. The other awards are the Luftwaffe Flak Badge and the Silver Wound Badge. *Author.*

The same tunic but this time the Iron Cross ribbon is worn through the second buttonhole, as per regulations. *Author.*

The ribbon bar in wear as per regulations. The ribbons are those of the Iron Cross 2nd Class 1939, Russian Front Medal and the Rumanian Anti Communist Service Medal. *Author.*

much photographic evidence of ribbon bars being worn on all manner of uniforms by members of all the armed services and para-military organisations that abounded during the period from 1933-1945.

Ribbon bars were a means for the individual to show what decorations that he or she had earned during his or her military service when circumstances didn't allow for the wearing of the full medals. German personnel wore all of their war badges into the field. This was practical because these badges were designed to be worn on all occasions-medals by their nature are not as robust as war badges and it would not be practical for your average panzer driver or fallschirmjäger to go into action wearing a full medal bar on their uniform. There is much photographic evidence from World War II that shows German military personnel wearing ribbon bars in many different situations. From *Gefreiter* to *Feldmarschall*, many wore ribbon bars on their uniforms as a testimony to their service for the Fatherland. Some might think it pretentious to wear all one's decorations in the field but anyone who understands what it is like to serve in the military, or how the military mind works, will appreciate the importance attached to the medals and awards that a country bestows upon its military personnel as well as the morale factor for civilians to see well decorated soldiers on the propaganda newsreels such as *Die Woche* and *Pathé News* (two of the well-known wartime weekly news programmes that kept the German and British public abreast of events respectively.)

A Volkssturm officer wearing a combination of World War I and II awards. The ribbon bar consists of the Iron Cross 2nd Class 1914 and the Cross of Honour 1914-1918. The War Merit Cross 2nd Class, either with or without Swords, is worn in the second buttonhole of the tunic. *Courtesy of Franco Mesturini.*

Untersturmführer Erich Zepper of the Waffen-SS Division 'Das Reich' wearing an impressive array of awards. As well as his Knights Cross, Iron Cross 1st Class, Close Combat Clasp in Bronze, Infantry Assault Badge in Silver and Wound Badge in Black, his ribbon bar consists of the ribbons of the Iron Cross 2nd Class, Russian Front Medal, SS Long Service Medal and the medals of 13-3-1938 and 1-10-1938. This officer has obviously seen a lot of pre-war service as indicated by the Flower War medals and the long service award. *Courtesy of Justin Horgan.*

two

Construction

As with all original Third Reich militaria, ribbon bars were made to very high standards. Even a single ribbon bar of the lowliest award was made to exacting and strict regulations. The following photographs show a selection of the different ribbon bars that may be encountered.

The first ribbon shown (below) is a single ribbon bar of the Iron Cross 2nd Class. The ribbon is 25mm long and 17mm high. The ribbon is folded over the metal convex backing plate, stitched down and backed by grey wool. Blue and black wool can also be encountered, as can a bare shiny metal plate. The ribbon bar is attached to the uniform by a pin that is clipped into either a small hook or a curved receiver.

The second ribbon shown (below) is of the style most commonly seen in photographs, and encountered by collectors. The dimensions of this ribbon are as follows; each medal ribbon is 15mm long and 17mm high. The construction is the same as the previous bar. The awards on this ribbon bar are as follows; War Merit Cross 2nd Class with Swords, Russian Front Medal, Army/Kriegsmarine 4 Year Long Service Medal.

The third ribbon shown is the less common 30mm ribbon bar. It is also 17mm long. This example has no wool backing on the reverse. The example shown is the Medal of the 1st of October 1938, Sudetenland Medal, with the Prague Castle Bar.

The fourth ribbon shown (below) is different from No.2 only in that it is 11mm high as opposed to the more common 17mm encountered. Each ribbon is 15mm long as per normal with these kind of ribbon bars. This example clearly shows the bare backing plate often encountered. The awards on this ribbon bar are as follows; Iron Cross 2nd Class 1914, Baden Military Service Cross, 1914-1918 Cross of Honour for Combatants.

The fifth example shown (below) is the sew on type of ribbon bar that was favoured by older officers in the German military of the time. Each ribbon is as usual, 15mm long, and 10mm high. The ribbons are folded over a hard backing and sewn down, and backed with cloth. The ribbon would then be sewn onto the tunic, thus negating the need for the usual loops found on tunics that have ribbon bars. The awards on this ribbon bar are as follows; Iron Cross 2nd Class 1914, with the 1939 Bar miniature, Russian Front Medal, Hamburg Hansa War Cross, 1914-1918 Cross of Honour for Combatants, Army 25 Year Service Cross, Army 18 Year Service Cross, Tirol Service Medal.

The sixth ribbon bar shown (below) is a style that is occasionally encountered. The dimensions are the same as the ribbon bar in figure 2. The difference is that two lengths of each ribbon are used in what is known as the "Austrian Fold". The method of construction is identical to that of the other pin-back ribbon bars. The awards shown are as follows; Iron Cross 2nd Class 1939, Luftwaffe 4 Year Long Service Medal, Medal of the 13th of March, 1938, the Annexation of Austria, Medal of 1st of October 1938, with Prague bar.

The seventh (below) and eighth bars shown are two variations of the same style. The seventh ribbon bar is of the same dimensions as ribbon bar No.2 above. The difference is that the wearer of this ribbon bar displays miniatures of all of his awards on the ribbon bar. The awards are; the Iron Cross 2nd Class 1914, World War I Wound Badge in Silver, and the Cross of Honour 1914-1918. This practice gained popularity again after 1957 when German veterans were permitted to wear de-nazified versions of awards won in the Second World War. Photographs of these veterans in Bundeswehr uniforms show them wearing ribbon bars that have miniatures of all of their awards.

The eighth ribbon bar shown (below) is of the same dimensions as the first bar shown in this section and displays the larger sized miniature that can be found on ribbon bars of the period, the miniatures being the Iron Cross 2nd Class 1914 and the Cross of Honour 1914-1918. These eight different examples are shown purely to give a general idea of the shape, construction, and style of ribbon bar that may be encountered. As with most German awards, variations do exist and this list does not claim to be exhaustive. However, the average ribbon you may encounter will generally conform to the dimensions and construction described and pictured above.

The photograph on page 24 shows how ribbons were manufactured. The awards shown are that of the Iron Cross 2nd Class 1939 and the War Merit Cross 2nd Class with or without Swords in an uncut strip, alongside a completed ribbon bar, and examples of the awards. The ribbon would be cut to size, folded over the backing plate and stitched down, and then backed either with metal and/or wool. If the recipient of the ribbon bar was a holder of the War Merit Cross with Swords, then a miniature crossed swords device would be affixed to the corresponding ribbon by means of two narrow folding pins, as illustrated in the photograph.

three

How to Decipher German Ribbon Bars

Regulations were laid down as to the correct order in which ribbons were to be worn on the ribbon bar. The order of importance is listed below. However, there are differing opinions as to where some awards are actually placed, such as the medals that were awarded pre-war, for example the Social Welfare award, and the medals awarded by Spain to the German forces that took part in the Civil War. I have not gone into the awards of the Veterans associations in any great detail, as most of these awards were worn as a pin-back award. The exceptions to this are the Baltic Cross (awarded for Freikorps service in 1919). It has a white ribbon with a blue central stripe and two thin blue stripes. The second award is the Silesian Eagle 2nd Class (an unofficial award which later became an official award, which was originally awarded for the defence of Silesia in 1919-1920). It has a ribbon of pale yellow with a central white stripe. The Baltic Cross was more popular in its medal form, whereas the Silesian Eagle 2nd Class is more likely to be encountered on the ribbon bar. The Silesian Eagle ranks above the Baltic Cross but both rank below military awards.

I have attempted to be as accurate as possible but do not claim to be all-knowing in this matter.

1. Iron Cross 2nd Class 1939 or Iron Cross 2nd Class 1914 with or without the 1939 Bar attached to the 1914 ribbon. (Eisernes Kreuz 2nd Klasse) This award ranked above all other awards and could be worn either on the ribbon bar, medal bar or in the second buttonhole of the tunic. The EKII 1914 has a ribbon that has a black centre stripe bordered by thin white stripes, which in turn are bordered by thin black stripes. The ribbon of the EKII 1939 differed in that the central stripe is red, to commemorate the sacrifice of Germany's youth in the Great War. (top page 26)

Four ribbon bar consisting of the Iron Cross 2nd Class 1939, War Merit Cross 2nd Class with Swords, Russian Front Medal, Army/Navy 12 Year Long Service Medal. *Author.* **£25/$42**.

2. War Merit Cross 2nd Class with or without Swords. (Kriegsverdienst Kreuz) Method of wear is the same as above. It ranked next to the Iron Cross. A combat award is distinguished on the ribbon bar by the affixing of a pair of crossed swords. (The War Merit Medal, usually awarded to civilians, is distinguished on the ribbon bar by a thin red stripe running down the centre of the black stripe. It ranked well below the other classes of the War Merit awards.)

3. Social Welfare Medal with or without Swords. Wartime regulations specified that the German Social Welfare decoration could not be awarded to military personnel if their service qualified them for an award of the War Merit Cross or some other military award. It continued to be awarded in an honourary manner. It can be found on ribbon bars that belong to someone with pre-war service. (below)

Six ribbon bar consisting of the Iron Cross 2nd Class 1939, Social Welfare Medal, Army/Navy 4 and 12 Year Long Service Medals, Olympic Games Commemorative Medal and the Medal of 1-10-1938 with Prague Bar. *Author.* **£60/$100**.

4. Russian Front Medal. (Medaille Winterschlacht im Osten.) This medal was awarded to commemorate the 1st Winter campaign in Russia in 1941-1942 but continued to be awarded for service after those dates. It was usually worn either through the second buttonhole of the tunic or on the ribbon bar. The sacrifice in Russia was reflected in the esteem in which this award was held and ranked highest of all campaign awards.

5. 1914-1918 Cross of Honour with or without Swords. (Ehrenkreuz 1914-1918.) Commonly known as the Hindenburg Cross, it was awarded in recognition of World War I service. Front-line service is distinguished on the ribbon bar by a pair of crossed swords whilst non combatants wore the same ribbon without swords. The Cross of Honour for Widows and Next of Kin were usually presentation pieces, but I possess a ribbon bar of the award. It differs greatly form the other ribbons in that it is a white ribbon with a red stripe running down the centre, flanked by two black stripes. (below)

Five ribbon bar consisting of the Iron Cross 2nd Class 1914, War Merit Cross 2nd Class with Swords, 1914-1918 Cross of Honour with Swords, 25 Year Faithful Service Cross and the Westwall Medal. *Author*. **£30/$50**.

6. Life Saving Medal. (Rettungsmedaille.)As with the Social Welfare awards, after the outbreak of war, military personnel were more likely to be awarded the War Merit Cross instead of this award. There was confusion about where the medal should be placed and was often placed either after the Cross of Honour or after the service awards. The ribbon took the form of a yellow ribbon with white stripes on either side.

7. Wehrmacht Long Service Medals. (Wehrmacht Dienstauszeichnungen.) These awards came in four classes, with a further special class for forty years service. The 4th Class Silver Medal was awarded for four years service, the 3rd Class Gold Medal for twelve years, the 2nd Class Silver Cross for eighteen years and

the 1st Class Gold Cross for twenty-five years. The special forty year award was identical to the twenty-five year award but had the addition of golden Oakleaves on the cornflower blue ribbon. The ribbon was identical for all the classes of this award. When worn on the ribbon bar, long service awards of the Heer and Kriegsmarine were distinguished by a straight winged eagle, much like that worn on the uniform, and was in either silver or gold depending on the award held. A member of the Luftwaffe's long service award is distinguished by the Luftwaffe eagle, again in either silver or gold. Two awards could be worn at the same time, with the higher award taking precedence. The Wehrmacht Long Service awards ranked below combat decorations as well as the Russian Front Medal and the 1914-1918 Cross of Honour, but ranked above the 'Flower War' Medals and national awards. (below)

Single ribbon bar for the Army/Navy 4 Year Long Service Medal. *Author.* **£5/$8**.

8. 1936 Olympic Games Commemorative Medal. (Olympia-Erinnerungs-medaille.) Awarded in recognition of services rendered in the preparations and execution of the 1936 Berlin Olympic Games. The medal ranked below the service awards but above the 1938-1939 occupation awards.

9. NSDAP and other long service awards i.e. Civil, SS, Polizei, Customs, RAD, Fire Service, etc.

NSDAP awards (Dienstauszeichnungen der NSDAP.) The party had three classes of award, which could be all worn at the same time. The 3rd Class 10 Year award in Bronze can be seen in the photograph at the top of page 29. The 2nd Class 15 Year award in Silver and the 1st Class 25 Year award in Gold are distinguished by a blue and silver ribbon and a red and off-white ribbon respectively. The Party miniature on the ribbon is identical in all classes except for its colour- Bronze. Silver and Gold respectively. These awards ranked below the military service awards, except with the SS, who wore them in front of their military service awards.

Four ribbon bar consisting of the War Merit Cross 2nd Class without Swords, NSDAP 10 Year Medal, Medal of 13-3-1938 and the Medal of 1-10-1938. *Courtesy of Bill Shea.* **£30-35/$50-60**.

SS long service awards (SS Dienstauszeichnungen) came in four classes which were as follows. A 4 Year Black Medal, an 8 Year Bronze Medal, a 12 Year Silver Cross, and a 25 Year Gold Cross. These awards were worn on the ribbon bar in the form of a plain cornflower blue ribbon in the case of the 4 and 8 Year Medals. In the case of the 12 and 25 year Service Crosses, again a plain blue ribbon was worn but with the addition of an SS miniature runes on the ribbon in Silver or Gold respectively. Only the highest class could be worn at one time unless the recipient held an award for military service. (below)

Three ribbon bar consisting of the Iron Cross 2nd Class 1939, SS 12 Year Long Service Cross, Spanish Civil War Campaign Medal. As with most SS militaria, there are more fakes than original items on the market. I believe this ribbon bar to be correct but would welcome comment from other collectors. *Author.* **£75/$125**.

Polizei long service awards (Polizei Dienstauszeichnungen) came in three classes. The 3rd Class 8 Year Medal which, when worn on the ribbon bar, was a plain ribbon with no miniature, the 2nd Class 18 Year Silver Cross which, when worn on the ribbon bar, was again a blue ribbon but with the addition of a miniature Polizei symbol in Silver, the 1st Class 25 Year Gold Cross, which was worn in the same manner as the Second Class on the ribbon bar but the miniature Polizei device was in Gold. As with the SS awards, if the Policeman held any military awards, wear all the Polizei awards he was entitled to. Polizei awards were ranked below military awards. (top of page 30)

Four ribbon bar consisting of the Iron Cross 2nd Class 1939, Russian Front Medal, Polizei 18 Year Long Service Cross, Westwall Medal. *Author.* **£30-35/$50-60**.

The Fire Service Cross (Feuerwehr Ehrenzeichen.) was awarded for 25 years service and had a red/white/red ribbon edged with black.

The Custom Service award (Zollgrenzschutz-Ehrenzeichen) was a Bronze Cross given for 4 years service. It also has the cornflower blue ribbon and on the ribbon bar had a miniature of the Custom Service symbol in Bronze. (below)

An impressive bar that spans both wars. The eight ribbons are the Iron Cross 2nd Class 1914 for non-combatants, Prussian Order of the Red Eagle 3rd/4th Class, Long Service Medal, Austrian Order of Leopold, 1914-1918 Cross of Honour with Swords, Customs 4 Year Service Medal, Luftschutz Medal, Westwall Medal. Some of the Imperial awards may have been incorrectly identified but every attempt has been made to be correct. *Author.* **£70/$115**.

Faithful Service Decorations (Treudienst Ehrenzeichen) were awarded to civilians for exemplary service to Germany through their work or outstanding faithfulness to duty. There were three classes, 25 Year in Silver, 40 Year in Gold, and a special 50 Year award. On the ribbon bar, this award was denoted by a cornflower blue ribbon with a miniature of the medal on the ribbon, in the colour of the grade being held at the time.

RAD awards (Dienstauszeichnungen fur den Reichsarbeitsdienst) came in four classes; 4th class Bronze Medal for four years service, 3rd Class Silver Medal for twelve years service, 2nd Class Silver Medal for eighteen years service, and a 1st Class Gold Medal for twenty-five years service. There are a number of RAD ribbon bars that may turn up but most are rare due to the short life span they had in the 1933-1945 period. At first a miniature of the Gold medal was affixed to the usual cornflower blue ribbon to indicate the twenty-five year award and the same in

Silver to indicate the eighteen year award. The lower classes were denoted by a plain, unadorned ribbon, as in the case of the Polizei and the SS. There then followed a revision of this and a miniature of the RAD insignia was authorised for wear on the ribbon bar. However, this was again reviewed after only three months. From late 1940 until the end of the war, a small national emblem was used in Gold and Silver for the 1st and 2nd Class awards respectively, and again the 3rd and 4th class were represented by the plain service ribbon.

As can be seen from the above list, ribbon bars with plain blue ribbons have the potential to be more interesting than they may appear at first glance.

10. Medal of 13-3-1938; (Austrian Anschluss. Medaille zur erinnerung an den 13-3-38). Awarded to all personnel, military and non military who took part in the peaceful occupation of Austria which began on 13 March 1938.

11. Medal of 1-10-1938; (Sudetenland, with or without Prague Bar. Medaille zur erinnerung an den 1-10-38). The medal was awarded for the occupation of the Sudetenland in Czechoslovakia after the Munich Accord signed by the Allies and Germany, with Italy as an observer. The medal with the Prague Bar, was awarded to all personnel who took part in occupying the rest of Czechoslovakia, being Bohemia and Moravia. The Bar was instituted on May 1st, 1939.

12. Medal of 23-3-1939; (Memelland Medal. Medaille zur erinnerung an die Heimkehr des Memellandes). Awarded to commemorate the return of the Memelland to Germany from Lithuania. It was the last of the Occupation medals to be awarded. It is also the rarest as only a small number of German personnel were involved. (below)

A selection of single ribbon bars for the Flower War medals to commemorate the pre war German expansion in Europe. They are called the Flower War medals due to the largely bloodless invasions that led to Germany taking territory claimed to be rightfully theirs. The ribbons are, from left to right; Medal of 13-3-1938. **£5/$8**; Medal of 1-10-1938. **£5/$8**; Medal of 1-10-1938 with Prague Bar. **£15/$25**; Medal of 23-3-1939. **£10/$16**. *Author.*

13. Awards of the German Red Cross. (Deutsches Rotes Kreuz, DRK). There were many awards given by the DRK during the time of the Third Reich. However, the only ones that are relevant to this work are the 2nd Class Cross of the DRK and the Medal of the DRK, both of which had a red and white ribbon. They ranked below all other service awards and the photograph below shows the DRK medal in wear.

Hauptmann Franz Kielich displays a fine array awards in this wartime colour photograph, which allows us to see what may well be the DRK decoration on the end of the ribbon bar. *Courtesy of Justin Horgan.*

14. Luftschutz Awards; The 2nd Class Medal and 1st Class Cross were awarded to those who had served with distinction in the civil defence of Germany since 1933. The awards were rendered to a wide range of personnel. Both the 1st and 2nd Class could be worn simultaneously on the ribbon bar but had no miniature to identify one from the other. However, it is presumed that the higher award would come first on the ribbon bar. This award ranked below the military service awards. (below)

A single ribbon bar of the Luftschutz award. *Author*. **£5/$8**.

15. Defence Wall Medal (Westwall Medal. Deutsches Schutzwall-Ehrenzeichen.) Awarded for service in the defence of Germany, and in particular the construction of the Siegfried Line before and shortly after the outbreak of the war. It was awarded again later in the build-up of Germany's defences after 1942, especially on the Atlantic Wall, which was part of Festung Europa. When worn on the ribbon bar, it ranked below the service awards.

16. Foreign Awards i.e. Spain, Italy, Hungary, Bulgaria, Finland, Croatia, etc. German soldiers were often decorated by the grateful leaders of the Axis powers. There are many photographs of German soldiers wearing Finnish, Croatian, Eastern Peoples awards, and so on. I take a risk by putting the Spanish Civil War awards in this position also. I have seen and heard opinions that give the Spanish awards a far higher importance than I do. I do not claim greater knowledge than anyone else and would welcome comment on this point. I place the Spanish awards with the other foreign awards because from the ribbon bars I own and others that I have seen, all place the Spanish awards at the end of the ribbon bar. As can be seen in this photograph, the Spanish awards most frequently seen on German ribbon bars are the Spanish Red Military Cross and/or the Campaign Medal, with and without Swords. (top of page 34)

Four ribbon bar consisting of the Iron Cross 2nd Class 1939, War Merit Cross 2nd Class without Swords, Spanish Red Military Cross and the Spanish Civil War Campaign Medal. *Author*. **£40/$65**.

It is important to mention Imperial awards at this point. There were a vast number of awards to which German and Austrian soldiers were entitled to during the First World War, far too many to list here. Some Imperial awards may be found on ribbon bars directly behind the Iron Cross 2nd Class. However, other Imperial awards rank below awards rendered by Germany during the Third Reich period. Those who held middle to senior officer rank in the First World War tended to wear a lot of Imperial awards on their Third Reich ribbon bar, whereas lower ranks tended to have only the Iron Cross 2nd Class and the Cross of Honour 1914-1918. (below)

Five ribbon bar example of a combined Imperial and Third Reich set of awards. They are the Iron Cross 2nd Class 1914, War Merit Cross 2nd Class with Swords, Russian Front Medal, Bavarian Military Service Cross, 1914-1918 Cross of Honour with Swords. *Author.* **£35/$55-60**.

To decipher a ribbon bar, one must always start from left to right. Ribbon bars may be encountered that have ribbons in the incorrect order. This does not necessarily mean that they are fake. It could simply be that whoever made the ribbon bar was not up to speed on the correct order of importance of the medals or could have been having a bad day.

Take the following ribbon bar for example (top page 35). As you can see from the photograph, the ribbon for the Medal of 1-10-1938, is in the incorrect position. It should be after the service awards on the ribbon bar so instead of the order that

we see in the photograph, the order should be War Merit Cross with swords, Luftwaffe 12 and 4 Year Long Service Medals, Medal of 1-10-1938, Luftschutz Medal. Some people tend to be nervous of awards or medals that do not conform exactly with the manufacturer's examples that are well known. However, I personally like to get the occasional ribbon bar that does not have the correct order, providing that it is an *original* item. I also have a number of examples of the same bar and it is always handy to have spares for swaps for a different example that may turn up at a militaria show or on a list.

four

Ribbons of the Famous

The following photographs show two of the many varieties of combinations that may be encountered on German ribbon bars. Many examples have a mixture of both Imperial and Third Reich period decorations. Some people prefer to buy ribbon bars with only Third Reich ribbons but this, whilst entirely up to the individual, denies one the pleasure of some of the longer and more interesting ribbon bars that reflect service from 1914-1945. There are ribbon bars with one, two, three, anywhere up to twelve ribbons. (two below)

Six ribbon bar consisting of the Iron Cross 2nd Class 1939, War Merit Cross 2nd Class with Swords, Russian Front Medal, Army/Navy 4 Year Long Service Medal, Medal of 13-3-1938, Medal Of 1-10-1938 with Prague Bar. This bar is said to have come from a high ranking officer. Unfortunately, that is all the information that came with it when it was purchased. *Author.* **£55/$90**.

Five ribbon bar consisting of the Iron Cross 2nd Class 1939, War Merit Cross 2nd Class with Swords, Russian Front Medal, Army/Navy 12 & 4 Year Long Service Medals. *Author.* **£45/$75**.

In some cases ribbon bars have even more; a good example of a long ribbon bar is that of *SS-Oberstgruppenführer* Sepp Dietrich, whose personal ribbon bars amounted to well over eighteen ribbons and necessitated the wearing of two bars! Grossadmiral Dönitz also wore his extensive ribbon bar in this manner, as this official portrait photograph shows clearly (above). Generally the ribbon bars en-

countered by collectors will number anywhere from one to three, up to eight awards. It is the truly lucky collector who comes across a long original bar at a militaria show, but this can happen. I know of one collector, a good friend of mine, who has recently purchased a ribbon bar belonging to *Feldmarschall* Erwin Rommel, a photograph of which is shown above. The colour wartime postcard photograph of the "Desert Fox" (opposite), shows the same ribbon bar being worn. To find a piece like this doesn't happen very often as those who have collected for some time know only too well!

five

Reproduction Ribbon Bars

While the whole area of ribbon bar collecting has been largely overlooked by the ever-present fakers, there are however a number of reproduction ribbon bars on the market and one should be on the alert as to what they look like and their construction. The majority of reproductions that I have encountered to date tend to be of the longer ribbon bar i.e. with at least six or more awards. The following photograph shows two of the better fakes on the market. The top ribbon bar has

twelve awards – quite a find if it was original! The order in which the awards are on the bar is correct, indeed some of the miniatures on the bar are, I believe to be original. On the whole, what lets the whole thing down is the size and quality of the Prague Bar miniature on the Sudetenland ribbon, third last from the end. It is totally unlike any other Prague Bar miniature seen to date and is very crudely finished.

The second ribbon bar at first looks to be correct. However, there are a number of things wrong with it. The first is the order of the awards. I stated earlier in the book that some awards were put in the wrong order due to ignorance or by accident. I find it hard to believe that anyone least of all a German soldier with such obvious long service, would wear a ribbon bar in such obvious wrong order. The occupation medals should be after the long service awards, and the Russian Front Medal and KVK 2nd Class should be next to the Iron Cross 2nd Class 1914. There is also the absence of the Cross of Honour for Combatants 1914-1918 to

consider. Anyone with the Iron Cross 2nd Class 1914 was entitled to the Cross of Honour as well. As with the first bar we looked at, the Prague Bar lets down this ribbon bar as it is also a crudely attempted copy. The ribbon for the War Merit Cross 2nd Class is actually a War Merit Medal ribbon that has had the red stripe in the centre coloured in by a black felt-tip pen. Finally, as can be seen in the photograph below showing the reverse of the ribbon bar, the back of the ribbon is poorly and incorrectly finished, with a piece of red felt glued in place. Some of the miniatures on this ribbon bar are original but overall, there is just too much wrong with the ribbon bar for it to be an original wartime piece.

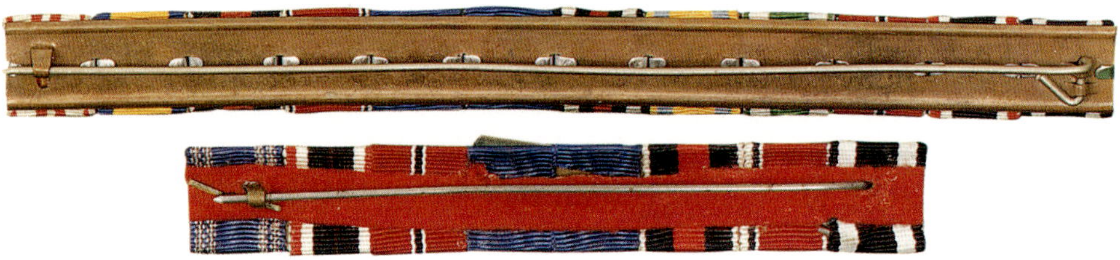

It is interesting to note that the reverse of the longer ribbon bar is actually in keeping with an original bar and may be constructed from spare original components picked up after the war. To buy original ribbon bars of this size and quality would represent a sizable outlay of expense for the collector. Perhaps that is why the reproducers have concentrated on the longer ribbon bars or more unusual ones i.e. with SS runes. However, I have come across some smaller ribbon bars which were also fake, the most recent being the 1st Class NSDAP Long Service award on a one inch ribbon bar. This would be quite a catch for a collector but when closely examined, the golden miniature party device was poorly made and the construction of the ribbon bar, which looked good from a distance, was very shoddy when closely examined.

This section on fakes does not claim to be exhaustive or all-knowing. There are many people out there with much more knowledge on the matter. All I have attempted to do here is to pass on the fruits of my own experiences and mistakes, some of which were costly! Reproduction German militaria is all too commonplace, from the crude attempts to items that are better made than some of the originals. As with buying any militaria, if there is any doubt in your mind <u>do not buy</u> the item because your initial reaction is usually correct. Always make sure that the person you are buying from has a money-back guarantee approach to selling militaria. Beware anyone who answers your question, "Is this original?" with the reply, "It's original to me!" Such an ambiguous answer speaks volumes as to that

dealer's attitude to the buying public. Never be afraid to ask the advice of a fellow collector or dealer you trust and know to have more knowledge than you about militaria. We all started out with very little knowledge and most collectors will speak well of fellow collectors who saved them a lot of money in the early days of their collecting.

six

The Men Behind the Ribbons

Ribbon bars, like a good deal of militaria, tend to be anonymous in that it is hard to find the history attached to them. Unless the collector can obtain the ribbon bar or medals from either a veteran or from the veteran's family, or unless the seller has the provenance of the item, the "man behind the medal" is lost forever to history. Discovering the history attached to a ribbon bar can turn an ordinary piece of Militaria into a prize possession in a collection. Take for example the following photograph of an EKII, Russian Front Medal, the corresponding cita-

tions and ribbon bar. One of the most common ribbon bars on the market today is the EKII and Russian Front Medal. This is due to the high number of soldiers on the Eastern Front, not that the awards were easily won, contrary to Allied propaganda of the time. The human cost related to these awards is hard to quantify. A ribbon bar of these awards is worth about eight dollars on its own but in the case of the example shown above the value is increased because the ribbon bar is still with the rest of the individual soldiers awards.

These awards were won by *Unteroffizier* Eugen Giesing of the 5. Luftwaffe Flak Abteilung I 29 (Mot.) whilst serving on the Russian Front in 1941-1942. Herr Giesing was born in Solingen on the 22nd of September, 1919. He received his call-up on the 12th of July 1939, and entered military service on the 20th of October 1939 with the 4. Batterie Flak Ausbildungstelle at Kassel/Wolfsanger. After basic training he was transferred to the 5. Flak Abteilung I.29 (Mot) on the 12th of January 1940. During duties in defence of the Reich, which lasted until May 1940, he took part in the invasion of the Low Countries and the Battle of France. After France had fallen, the newly promoted Gefreiter Giesing was stationed back in Germany on air defence duties, having amassed 149 days in action against the Allies.

On the 22nd of June 1941, *Gefreiter* Giesing (below), along with three million of his Kameraden and Axis allies, crossed the border into the Soviet Union in the opening stages of Operation Barbarossa. He served from this date on the Eastern Front until his war service ended due to severe leg wounds received as the result of a grenade explosion during combat with Russian troops. During his service on the Eastern Front, this young flak gunner was awarded the Iron Cross 2nd Class 1939

Obergefreiter Eugen Giesing pictured beside a 2cm Flak gun. He and his comrades are wearing a variety of garments to fend off the fierce weather faced by the German forces in their first winter in Russia. *Author.*

on the 16th September 1941. He was again promoted in November 1941 to the rank of *Obergefreiter*. He was wounded on the 10th December 1941, for which he was awarded the Wound Badge in Black in the field hospital on the 13th of December, 1941 (right). However, *Obergefreiter* Giesing's war was about to come to an end.

As a result of injuries to the upper and lower right leg from a grenade blast a few days later, during combat in Terajewa on the 16th December 1941, *Obergefreiter* Giesing was evacuated back to Germany where he was hospitalised and spent almost the next fourteen months in hospital and convalescence homes. During his recuperation, he received the other decorations which he had earned during his time on

Obergefreiter Giesing pictured in hospital whilst recuperating after being wounded in Russia. His ribbon bar can be seen in this photograph. His other awards are not visible. *Author.*

Another day of cold and danger begins for the men of a Luftwaffe Flak unit in Russia. The men have made up for the lack of proper snow camouflage uniforms by cutting up bedsheets and using them as a crude but effective white Zeltbahn (shelter quarter) *Author.*

A Waffen-SS Oberscharführer wearing the ribbons of the Iron Cross 2nd Class 1939 and Russian Front Medal. *Courtesy of Franco Mesturini.*

the Eastern Front. These were as follows; the Luftwaffe Flak Badge awarded on the 4th April 1942, the Russian front Medal awarded on the 5th August 1942, and he was awarded the Luftwaffe Ground Assault Badge on paper. I say this because whilst I have the form stating he was entitled to the badge on the 3rd September 1942, there is no record of the award in his Wehrpass. The flimsy confirming the entitlement to the award states that he took part in two actions against the enemy at Kunja over the 25th and 26th of August, 1941, and a third action at Terajewa on December 16th, 1941. Perhaps the award was rendered after Herr Giesing's medical discharge on the 12th April 1943. It sometimes happened that soldiers never received an actual award having been awarded it on paper. I think that this must be the case as I have all of *Unteroffizier* Giesing's awards and citations, as well as his ribbon bar and Wehrpass.

So the next time you see a small ribbon bar of one or two ribbons, don't be discouraged at the lack of awards because a man had to go through difficult times even to earn a small ribbon bar. Unfortunately, most ribbon bars come without any provenance but they each have a story and a price that was paid for through hardship and human suffering.

The following photographs are included to illustrate the variety of ribbon bars worn by German Servicemen in both World Wars and again after 1957.

A father and son pictured during World War I, both wearing the ribbon bar of the Iron Cross 2nd Class 1914. *Courtesy of Franco Mesturini.*

Above left: A veteran of World War I wears the single ribbon bar of the Iron Cross 2nd Class 1914 on his best suit. *Courtesy of Franco Mesturini.*

Above: A member of the German Red Cross pictured with his wife. This man has seen extensive service, as testified by his impressive ribbon bar. *Courtesy of Franco Mesturini.*

Left: A Marine Artillery NCO wears his World War I awards and illustrates the wearing of the ribbon of the Iron Cross 2nd Class 1914 through the second buttonhole of the tunic and on the ribbon bar at the same time. *Courtesy of Franco Mesturini.*

Above: Lieutenant Commander Siegmund, commanding officer of VP 1501 and Flotilla Adjutant of the 15th Coastal Defence Forces Flotilla, wearing the 1939 Bar to the Iron Cross 2nd Class 1914 on his tunic. It is interesting to note that he also has the Iron Cross ribbon on his ribbon bar. *Author.*

Above right: A Polizei Oberwachtmeister wearing an army Panzer wrap-over tunic with Polizei insignia. He wears a ribbon bar comprising the War Merit Cross 2nd Class with Swords and the Medal of the 1-10-1938. *Courtesy of Franco Mesturini.*

Right: A member of the Deutsches Arbeits Front (German Labour Front) wearing the Austrian fold style of ribbon bar. *Courtesy of Franco Mesturini.*

Above: Knight's Cross holder Oberfeldwebel Karl Lausch wears his ribbon bar on his parade tunic. Normally the full medal bar would be worn. One explanation could be that this is one of a number of photographs taken with different styles of awards being worn for each photograph. *Author.*

Above right: An Afrika Korps Oberfeldwebel wearing a ribbon bar with the awards of the War Merit Cross 2nd Class with Swords, Army 4 Year Long Service Medal and the Medal of 1-10-1938. *Courtesy of Franco Mesturini.*

Right: A Luftwaffe Oberst wearing the miniature 1939 Bar to the Iron Cross 2nd Class 1914 on his ribbon bar which is a combination of Imperial and Third Reich awards. *Courtesy of Franco Mesturini.*

A myriad of ribbon bar styles are seen in this photograph taken during the 1930s. the photograph can be dated to the mid-1930s because of the early SS uniform worn by the man third from the left and the Deutsches Luft Verband (the precursor of the Luftwaffe) officer second on the right. Note the manner in which the party official in the centre of the photograph wears the ribbon of the Iron Cross 2nd Class 1914. He has slipped the ribbon through the buttonhole of his tunic pocket on the left hand side. Both an unusual and illegal manner of wear! *Author.*

Above: A member of the Organisation Todt poses for the camera in his uniform, complete with the ribbon bar of the Iron Cross 2nd Class 1914 and the 1914-1918 Cross of Honour with Swords. Note the civilian shirt and tie – perhaps the photograph was a last minute idea? *Courtesy of Franco Mesturini.*

Above right: Knight's Cross holder and U-Boat Ace Wilhelm Domms wears the ribbons of the Iron Cross 2nd Class 1939, Navy 4 Year Long Service Medal and the Medal of 1-10-1938 over what is possibly an Italian bravery award. *Courtesy of Justin Horgan.*

Right: Waffen-SS Unterscharführer Günther Jahnke displays the manner in which the ribbons of the Iron Cross 2nd Class and Russian Front medals were worn together in the second buttonhole of the tunic. *Author.*

NSKK Gruppenführer Karl Eduard, Duke of Koburg, takes the salute in front of the massed ranks of the NSKK (National Socialist Motor Corps) and the Hitler Youth. He wears an impressive ribbon bar which may well have up to twelve awards. Also of note are his Golden NSDAP party badge and the DRK Service Cross. *Author.*

Above: Not everyone had lots of awards! This young soldier wears a single ribbon bar which is of the Westwall Medal. In spite of his lack of medals, this soldier has won the Infantry Assault Badge in Silver and the Wound Badge in Black. In order to hold these awards, this young man has engaged the enemy at least three times and has been wounded at least once. *Author.*

Above right: A very Prussian looking officer who has had a long military career which is testified to by his long ribbon bar which has at least twelve awards on it. The full medal bar must indeed have been quite impressive. *Courtesy of Franco Mesturini.*

Right: Knight's Cross holder Oberst Hugo Lauberau pictured in his Bundeswehr uniform and displaying the manner in which the 1957 awards were worn by Second World War veterans. *Courtesy of Justin Horgan.*

Above: A Panzer Oberfeldwebel wears the ribbon of the Russian Front Medal on the lapel of his Panzer tunic and his other awards on the ribbon bar. Some soldiers placed great importance on the Russian Front Medal in spite of it being regarded by some as the 'Order of the Frozen Flesh'. *Courtesy of Franco Mesturini.*

Above right: A Luftwaffe NCO who has seen extensive service in World War I. Indeed all of his awards both on the ribbon bar and the pin-back awards, apart from the Glider Badge and the 1914-1918 Cross of Honour, are Imperial awards. *Courtesy Of Franco Mesturini.*

Right: A Waffen-SS NCO wearing a long ribbon bar which again shows the older soldiers preference for the Austrian fold style of ribbon bar. *Courtesy of Franco Mesturini.*

A smiling Army officer poses for the camera wearing his World War I awards. Perhaps this is his first time back in uniform for a long time? *Author.*

Above: A picture can tell a thousand tales. This veteran of both wars displays the weariness of a soldier who has seen too much. As can be seen from his awards, (Iron Cross 2nd Class 1914, 1914-1918 Cross of Honour, Imperial Award, the Russian Front Medal and the Krim Armshield.) he is a veteran both of the trenches of World War I and the early fighting in Russia and the battles in the Crimea. *Courtesy of Franco Mesturini.*

Above right: Knight's Cross with Oakleaves holder Oberleutnant Wilhelm Niggermeyer appears in jovial mood. Perhaps he has heard of a promotion or has just received the Oakleaves to his Knight's Cross? He wears the small ribbon bar of the Iron Cross 2nd Class 1939 and the Russian Front Medal. This just goes to show what other awards can follow on from such a seemingly insignificant ribbon bar. Oberleutnant Niggermeyer has also been awarded two Individual Tank Destruction Badges. *Author.*

Right: Oberleutnant Karl Seibod of a Luftwaffe Field Division displaying a ribbon bar with the Iron cross 2nd Class 1939 and the War Merit Cross 2nd Class with Swords. Note the importance that this officer has attached to his Infantry Assault Badge in Silver, which he wears above his Iron Cross 1st Class. This was against regulations and all Luftwaffe Field Division personnel were expected to exchange the Army Infantry Assault Badge for the Luftwaffe Ground Assault Badge when it came into existence on 31-3-1942. *Courtesy of Georg Jagolski – 21 Lw. Felddivision via Kevin Conley Ruffner.*

appendix one

Lapel Ribbons and Miniature Awards

There is a further field of interest that should be addressed in a work on ribbon bars, namely the "Lapel Bows" that were worn by military personnel when in civilian dress. These "bows" are miniature ribbons constructed in the same way as the ribbons on ribbon bars only in a smaller form, which are then tied in a bow with the highest ranking decoration uppermost and then secured to a button which could be slipped into the buttonhole on the lapel of the civilian suit. There are many of these ribbon bows on the market today. To date, I have encountered a lot of examples that contain Imperial awards, along with the Cross of Honour 1914-1918 (Ehrenkreuz 1914-1918). Instituted by Reich President *Generalfeldmarschall* von Hindenburg on 13th July 1934 so therefore not an Imperial award but an award in recognition of service in the Great War.), and the series of service awards (Treudienst Ehrenzeichen) instituted by Adolf Hitler on 30th January 1938 to recognize loyal service by civilians to the German people. I have also encountered ribbon bows that are of post 1933 awards, such as the EKII 1939, the War Merit Cross 2nd Class with Swords, Russian Front Medal, Social Welfare, Luftschutz medal 2nd Class, and so on.

The following photographs illustrate some of the examples of ribbon bows most likely to be encountered at an average militaria show.

Ribbon Bow A is a miniature of the Cross of Honour 1914-1918 for Non-Combatants; an exact miniature of the full-sized award suspended from the correct ribbon tied in a bow and attached to a fabric covered button.

Ribbon Bow B is of the Faithful Service Cross 2nd Class in Silver for twenty-five years service; the ribbon of the award is surmounted by an exact miniature of the medal affixed directly to the centre of the bow with a simple button on the reverse.

Ⓐ

Ⓑ

Ribbon Bow C is a combination of military awards in order of seniority. The Cross of Honour 1914-1918 is uppermost, next is the Medal for Hungarian War Service, and finally the Medal for Bulgarian war Service. The three ribbons are tied in bow form and surmounted by a miniature crossed sword device which would indicate that the Cross of Honour 1914-1918 was for a combat veteran. This bow is again attached to a simple button on the reverse.

Ribbon Bow D is a combination of the Bavarian Military Service Cross and the Cross of Honour 1914-1918, again with a crossed swords indicating a combat veteran, and affixed to a small button on the reverse.

Ⓒ

Ⓓ

Ribbon Bow E is a combination of the Iron Cross 2nd Class 1914, Imperial Service award, Cross of Honour 1914-1918, tied with a length of the Cross of Honour ribbon and surmounted by crossed swords affixed to an ordinary button on the reverse. Bows C, D, and E are of the construction most likely to be encountered on the market today.

Ribbon Bow F is an unusual variation that hardly deserves the name bow. I have included it here because the ribbons used are of the same size as those in Ribbon Bow E. However with Bow F they are rolled tightly over a thin metal bar and stitched down. It is similar to a standard military ribbon bar but is much smaller. I would hazard a guess that it was owned by a man who wanted people to know very definitely that he had been a soldier. Another explanation could be quite simply that this was the style used by the military outfitter that the owner went to for a ribbon bow! The Assmann Catalogue of F.W. Assmann & Sohne of Ludenscheid illustrates four such lapel bars in its section on Imperial Awards. The ribbons on the "bow" are the Iron Cross 2nd Class 1914, Wurttemburg(?) Military Service Cross, and the Cross of honour 1914-1918. The small metal bar to which the ribbons are affixed are attached to a small metal disc.

(E)

(F)

These are only a small selection of the many lapel ribbons that are available. Whilst not ribbon bars in the strict sense, they are another form of military decoration and an interesting aside to the collecting of ribbon bars. Whilst they may not be desirable to every collector, they are inexpensive and have by and large been overlooked by the ever-present fakers, though I am sure that it will be only a matter of time before this will change.

Some may wonder why I have not included stick pins in this book. Stick pins only show miniatures of the award itself, and are therefore, beyond the scope of this book There are also miniatures of the awards that are suspended from a small ornamental chain and worn on the left lapel of the civilian suit. A good example of a stickpin in wear is in the following photograph of *Reichsmarschall* Göring taken in

1938. There are also miniatures of the awards which are suspended from the ribbon of the respective award. Examples of stick pins, medal chains, and miniature medals are all shown in the following photograph which illustrates the wide variety of these awards that are available to the collector. To elaborate on these awards any further is beyond the scope of this work but may be the subject of a further work at a later date.

A variety of miniatures, lapel bows and other miniatures that are on the market today. The ribbon bows are of the Iron Cross 2nd Class 1939, Social welfare Medal, Russian Front and Westwall Medals, Luftschutz Award, War Merit Cross 2nd Class with Swords, Westwall Medal. The miniatures are the Iron Cross 2nd Class 1914 and the Cross of Honour 1914-1918 on a chain, the Iron Cross 2nd Class 1939 and the Iron cross 2nd Class 1914. Also included are an Imperial ribbon bar on the original manufacturers price card which has a facsimile of the Iron Cross on it, a large ribbon bow for the 1870 Iron Cross, a commemorative ribbon bow, an Imperial long service ribbon bar and a 1957 pattern Paratroopers badge in its stick pin form. *Author.*

appendix two

1957 Awards

With the defeat of Germany and her remaining allies in 1945, the wearing of all Third Reich awards, decorations, and insignia was outlawed. As a result of this, it was an offence for German veterans to wear their wartime awards in public. Even wearing them at reunions was risky as these events were closely monitored for fear of a resurgence of Nazism in post-war Europe. This was the state of affairs until July 26th, 1957 when a proclamation was passed by the fledgling Bundesrepublik that allowed for replacement decorations and awards to be provided for the wartime veteran members of the newly formed Bundeswehr.

It was also permitted in this ruling for wartime veterans to apply for replacement awards, and to wear them. Only through this ruling were the many veterans of the German forces in World War II finally given state recognition. The 'new' awards were manufactured following where possible, the original wartime design. However, in all cases the swastika was removed and some awards also had the eagle removed from them as well. The other regulation that was passed regarding the wear of the 1957 awards is of importance to this work. This was the granting of permission for many of the awards to be worn in a ribbon bar form, including many awards that were not worn on the ribbon bars during World War II.

Qualification awards and combat related decorations were redesigned and reissued to veterans of the Army, Luftwaffe, Kriegsmarine, and Waffen-SS. The only awards to retain the eagle were those awarded to the Luftwaffe. As the photographs of Wartime veterans in Bundeswehr uniforms clearly illustrate, the preference was to wear most of the awards on the ribbon bar, including the Knight's Cross, German Cross in Gold, Iron Cross 1st and 2nd Class, the Wound Badge, the Close Combat Clasp and also the various arm shields. The larger pin-back awards could also be worn on the ribbon bar, on a Prussian blue ribbon, which is much darker than the wartime cornflower blue service ribbon. Many veterans reserved wearing their full-size Knight's Cross for formal occasions.

Left: Major Heinrich Wetjen wearing his Bundeswehr uniform and displaying an impressive array of awards on his ribbon bars. The awards worn are the Knight's Cross, German Cross in Gold, Iron Cross 1939 1st and 2nd Class, Close Combat Clasp in Bronze, Wound Badge in Gold, Infantry Assault Badge in Silver, Krim Shield and foreign awards. *Courtesy of Brendan Clarke.* Right: Oberst Schlicht wearing his ribbon bar whilst at a regimental dinner in the 1960s. *Author via Adolf Schlicht.*

A huge range of awards were reinstituted but quite a number remained outlawed by the new West Germany. These were any of the awards that were directly awarded by the Nazi party or had distinct political meaning, such as the Occupation (Flower War) medals of 1938-1939, Spanish Civil War awards, Mothers Crosses, Party service medals and so on.

Ribbon bars of the 1957 awards are quite collectible in their own right and belong in this book just as much as the Imperial ribbon bars of World War I and the Inter-War years. If one wishes to show the progression of military service during this period through the collecting of ribbon bars then the addition of at least one 1957 ribbon bar is a logical step. There are many 1957 period items on the market at the moment and the costs are relatively low. The awards were still being produced officially in Germany up until 4 years ago. The official production ceased at this time because the demand from serving soldiers had ceased because wartime veterans would all be on the retired list at this moment in time.

The following photograph shows two examples of the 1957 ribbon bars and awards that may be encountered by collectors. These were given to me by the renowned authority on German uniforms, Adolf Schlicht, whose own awards appear in this photograph, in the ribbon bar form. His awards are as follows; Iron

Cross First Class 1939, Iron Cross Second Class 1939, Close Combat Clasp in Bronze, Black Wound Badge, Infantry Assault Badge in Silver, DRL Sports badge. *Oberst* Schlicht is pictured at right wearing the miniature set of awards at a formal reception.

Author via Adolf Schlicht.

The photograph on page 66 shows a number of other 1957 ribbon awards, including both the pin back and sew-on variants. There is also a ribbon bar containing the Knight's Cross with Oakleaves and Swords, although this is incorrectly on an Iron Cross First Class ribbon-normally the ribbon for the Knight's Cross is somewhat larger when worn on the ribbon bar and would naturally take

precedence over all other awards being worn on the ribbon bar. As can be seen from the sew-on bar, the order of importance of some of the awards was changed with their re-institution in 1957. The wound badge appears to take greater precedence than the KVKII, the Russian Front Medal, and the General Assault badge, which was not the case during the war, as can be seen in the period photographs elsewhere in this book.

A selection of 1957 pattern ribbon bars. At the top of the picture is the Knight's Cross with Oakleaves and Swords on the ribbon of the Iron Cross. Below this is a pin-back ribbon bar comprising the Iron Cross 1st Class, Iron Cross 2nd Class, Close Combat Clasp in Bronze, Wound Badge in Black and the Infantry Assault Badge in Silver. Below this bar is the sew-on style of bar that is also encountered. The awards on this ribbon bar are the Iron Cross 1st and 2nd Classes, Wound Badge in Silver, General Assault Badge, War Merit Cross 2nd Class with Swords, Russian front Medal and what may be a Rumanian award. The last ribbon bar in this photograph is another pin-back bar which comprises the Iron Cross 2nd Class and the Wound Badge in Black. *Author via Oberst Adolf Schlicht.*

Bibliography

Angolia, John R., *For Führer and Fatherland - Military Awards of the Third Reich.* R. James Bender Publishing, San Jose, California, USA, 1989.

Angolia, John R., *For Fuhrer and Fatherland - Political and Civil Awards of the Third Reich.* R. James Bender Publishing, San Jose, California, USA, 1989.

Angolia, John R., and Schlicht, Adolf, *Uniforms and Traditions of the German Army, Volume 1,* R. James Bender Publishing, San Jose, California, USA, 1984.

Angolia, John R., and Schlicht, Adolf, *Uniforms and Traditions of the Kriegsmarine, Volume 1,* R. James Bender Publishing, San Jose, California, USA, 1989.

Angolia, John R., and Schlicht, Adolf, *Uniforms and Traditions of the Luftwaffe, Volume 1,* R. James Bender Publishing, San Jose, California, USA, 1996.

Davis, Brian L., *German Uniforms of the Third Reich 1933-1945,* Arms and Armour Press, London, 1980.

Hartung, Lothar, *Awards of the Third Reich*, Furstentum, Liechtenstein, 1981.

Hormann, Jörg M., *Uniformen der Panzertruppe, 1917 bis heute*, Podzun-Pallas, Friedberg, Germany, 1989.

Mollo, Andrew, *Uniforms of the SS, Collected Edition*, Windrow & Greene Publishing, London, England, 1997.

Purves, Alec A., *The Medals, Decorations and Orders of World War II,* J.B. Hayward & Son, Suffolk, England, 1986.

Ruffner, Kevin Conley, *Luftwaffe Field Divisions 1941-1945,* Osprey Publishing, London, England, 1990.

Scheibert, Horst, *Parades of the Wehrmacht 1934-1940*, Schiffer Publishing Ltd., Atglen, PA, USA, 1997.

U.S. War Department, *Handbook on German Military Forces,* Louisiana State University Press, Baton Rouge, USA, 1990.

Williamson, Gordon, *Infantry Aces of the Reich,* BCA Publishing, London, England, 1991.

Index

Luftwaffe vs. RAF: Flying Clothing of the Air War, 1939-45. Mick J. Prodger. An up-close and serious examination of the various patterns of flight jackets, suits, headgear and gloves worn by the courageous pilots and aircrews of these two great adversaries during WWII. This book includes a look at some of the more bizarre and experimental outfits as well as the standard flying kit for different climates and regions, with a special section on electrically-heated clothing. Also examined is the parallel development of flying clothing in the Luftwaffe and the Royal Air Force, and the surprising influence each country had upon the other. An invaluable reference source for collectors, re-enactors, artists, modellers, and historians.
Size: 9" x 12" • over 500 color and b/w photographs • 160 pp.
ISBN: 0-7643-0234-5 • hard cover • $49.95

Luftwaffe vs. RAF: Flying Equipment of the Air War, 1939-45. Mick J. Prodger. This second of a two volume study closely examines the development and uses of personal flying equipment of the Luftwaffe and RAF throughout WWII. From compasses secreted in tunic buttons, to floating rations, to suits with built-in parachutes, you'll find it all. All types of parachutes and harnesses, life preservers, inflatable boats, survival tools, weapons for self-defense, and even some of the paperwork and personal items carried by the airmen of these two opposing air forces. Study the sophisticated rescue and survival equipment available to Luftwaffe crews, alongside the clever, yet often brilliantly simple devices which enabled so many RAF flyers to evade capture.
Size: 9" x 12" • over 500 color and b/w photographs • 144 pp.
ISBN: 0-7643-0249-3 • hard cover • $49.95

Head Dress of the British Heavy Cavalry: 1842-1934. David JJ Rowe. Here is a book dedicated to the head-dress worn by the British Heavy Cavalry of the period 1842 to the present day. It is lavishly illustrated with both colour and black and white photographs of helmets, most of which have never previously been published. This book is an essential source of reference for both the established, and new collectors, and to the student of cavalry full dress uniforms of the period 1842-1934.
Size: 9" x 12" • 135 color and b/w photographs • 256 pp.
ISBN: 0-7643-0957-9 • hard cover • $75.00

German Paratroops: Uniforms, Insignia & Equipment of the Fallschirmjäger in World War II. Robert Kurtz. The uniforms and equipment of the elite German Fallschirmjäger is the subject of this detailed, illustrated study. Authentic items - smocks, dress tunics, boots, insignia, helmets, visor caps, gloves, knee pads and more - are shown in superb color photos, in both multiple full-view, and detail shots. Unpublished World War II era photos show uniforms and equipment being worn on a variety of war fronts. Also included is a short chapter covering other Axis airborne including Italian and Japanese gear.
Size: 9" x 12" • over 530 color and b/w photographs • 200 pp.
ISBN: 0-7643-1040-2 • hard cover • $59.95

U.S. Navy and Marine Corps Campaign & Commemorative Medals. Edward J. Emering. This work provides an in depth overview of not only the history and development of each campaign medal, but also the historical significance of the events surrounding the establishment of each medal. The book also covers several of the more important commemorative medals often struck on a limited basis to account for the lack of appropriate official federal awards. This work, which is well organized and easy to read, proves to be an interesting and informative reference work for the collector of these Navy and Marine Corps medals. A value guide is included.
Size: 8 1/2" x 11" • over 180 color and b/w photos • 88 pp.
ISBN: 0-7643-0386-4 • soft cover • $19.95

Camouflage Uniforms of the Soviet Union and Russia 1937-to the Present. Dennis Desmond. A comprehensive guide to the history, design and use of camouflage field uniforms of the Soviet Union and Russia. This excellent reference contains factual and interesting material covering the earliest days of uniform development to the most recent issues of the Ministry of Internal Affairs, former KGB and Spetsnaz forces. This book fills an important void in the collector reference library that has been vacant far too long. Designed with both the militaria collector and Russophile in mind, this book is an easy to use picture guide to the most sought after collectible in the Soviet and Russian militaria field, and is a must for any serious collector or intelligence analyst interested in the former Soviet Union or Russia.
Size: 8 1/2" x 11" • over 200 color photographs • 160 pp.
ISBN: 0-7643-0462-3 • hard cover • $45.00

Uniforms of the Soviet Union 1918-1945. David Webster & Chris Nelson. For the first time a photographic study of the Soviet uniforms from the Revolution, Civil War, Purges, and the Great Patriotic War. Hundreds of full color highly detailed photographs of actual uniforms are combined with period black and white photographs. Actual uniforms of Marshals of the Soviet Union, to private soldiers of all services are to be found in this extensive volume.
Size: 9" x 12" • over 500 color and b/w photographs • 288 pp.
ISBN: 0-7643-0527-1 • hardcover • $69.95

MiG Pilot Survival: Russian Aircrew Survival Equipment and Instruction. Alan R. Wise. *MiG Pilot Survival: Russian Aircrew Survival Equipment and Instruction* explores the components and details of Russian survival science with color photographs, in depth descriptions, and a full translation of the exact manual – with original illustrations intact – as used by Russian aircrews in time of crisis.
Size: 8 1/2" x 11" • over 180 color photographs and line drawings • 96 pp.
ISBN: 0-7643-0130-6 • hard cover • $19.95

Lenin's Legacy: A Concise History and Guide to Soviet Collectibles. Martin J. Goodman. *Lenin's Legacy* combines a concise history of the Soviet Union with a study of its "symbolism," which until now has largely been hidden from the West. The book shows nearly 2000 items including pins and badges, orders and medals, busts and statues, table medallions and wall plaques, banners and flags, paintings and coins and many others. Subjects covered include political, communist party, Aeroflot, Soviet space programs, party congresses, Lenin, Soviet military forces and others. This book is designed not only for the collector, but also the historian. Prices are included to aid collectors.
Size: 8 1/2" x 11" • over 900 color photographs • 208 pp.
ISBN: 0-7643-1019-4 • hard cover • 59.95

Also from the Publisher